Sid Did It

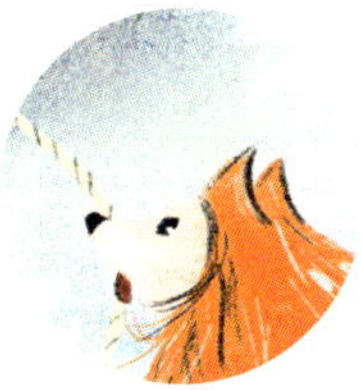

Written by
Stephen Rickard

Illustrated by
Tika and Tata

Ransom

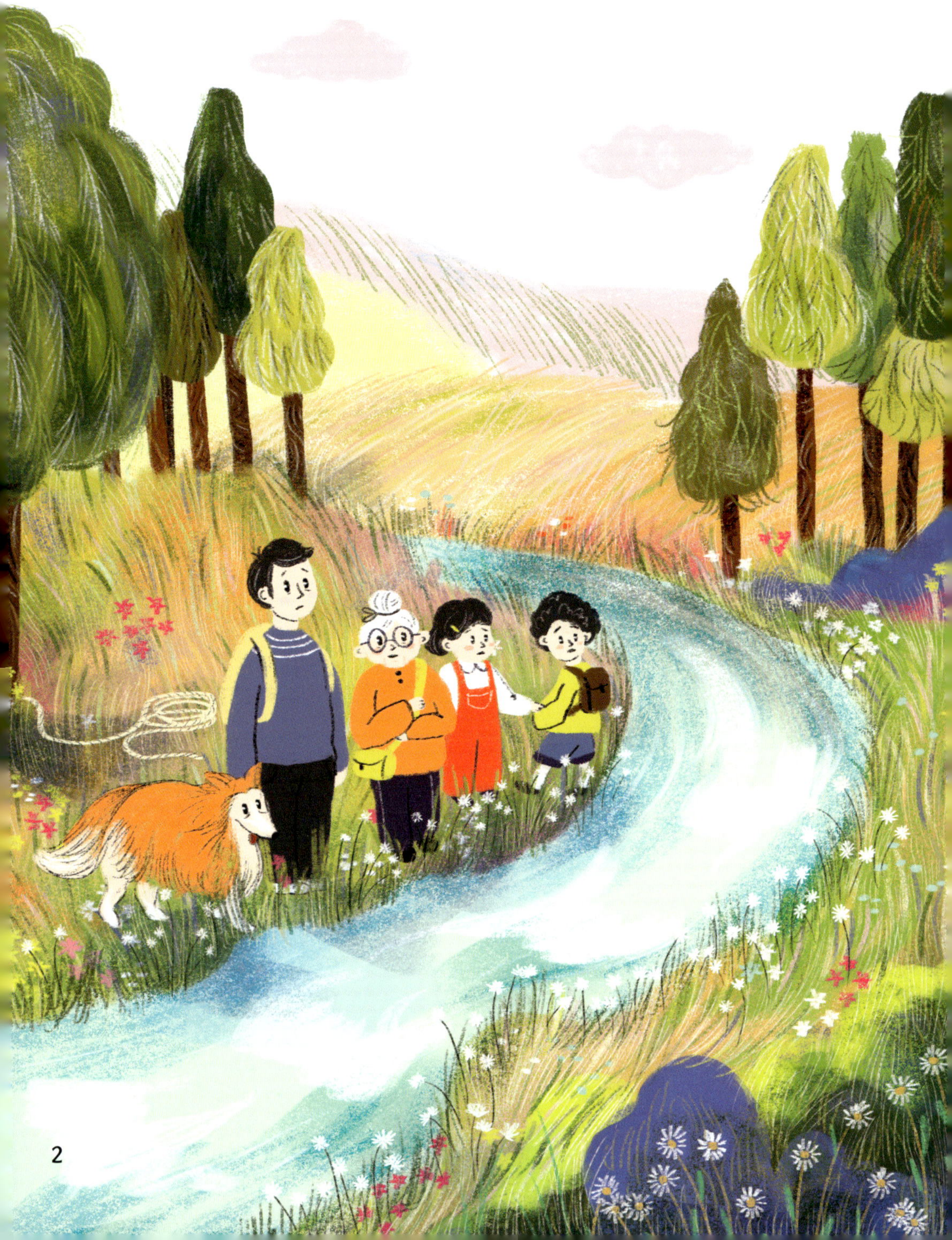

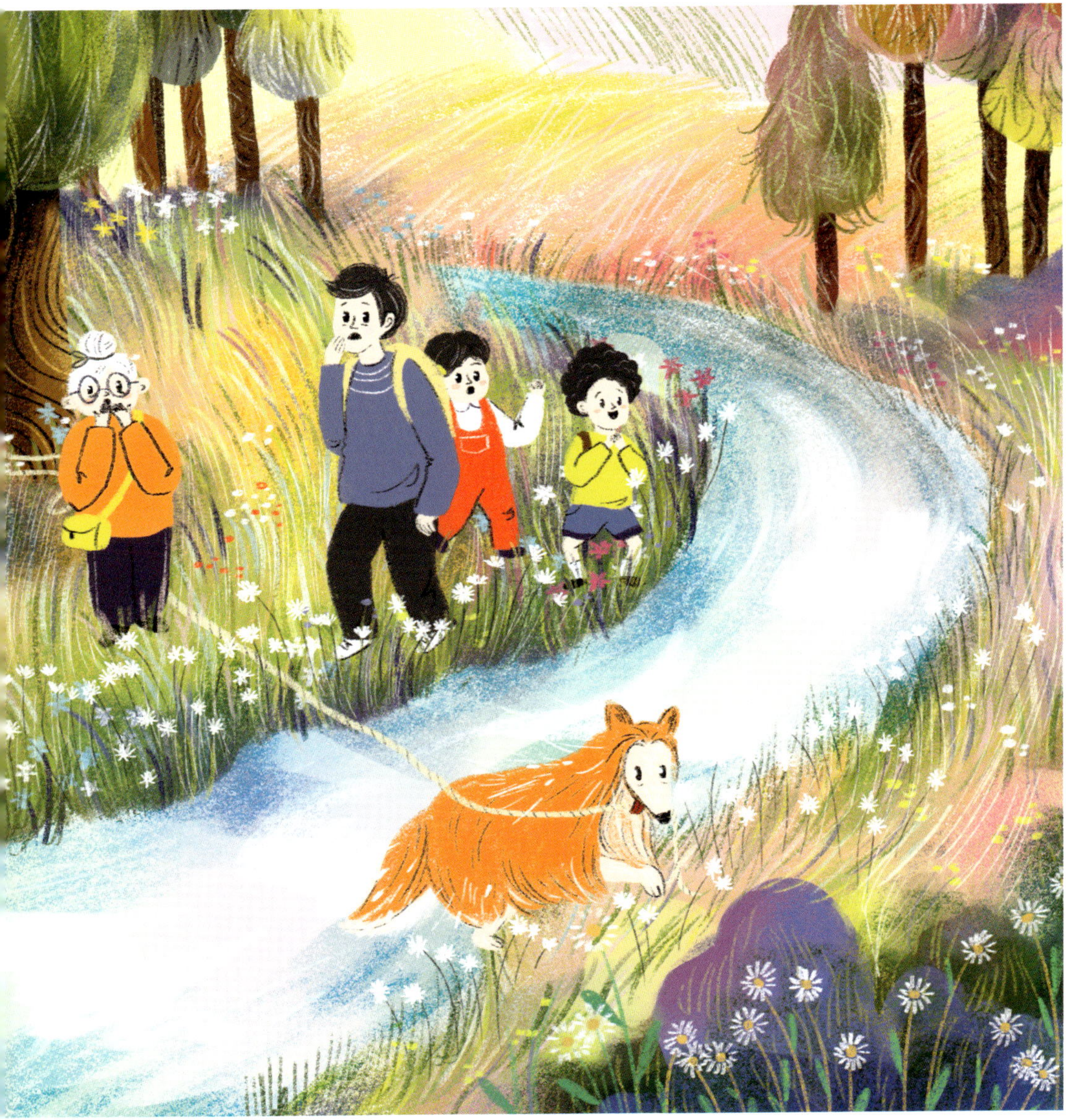

Sid did it.

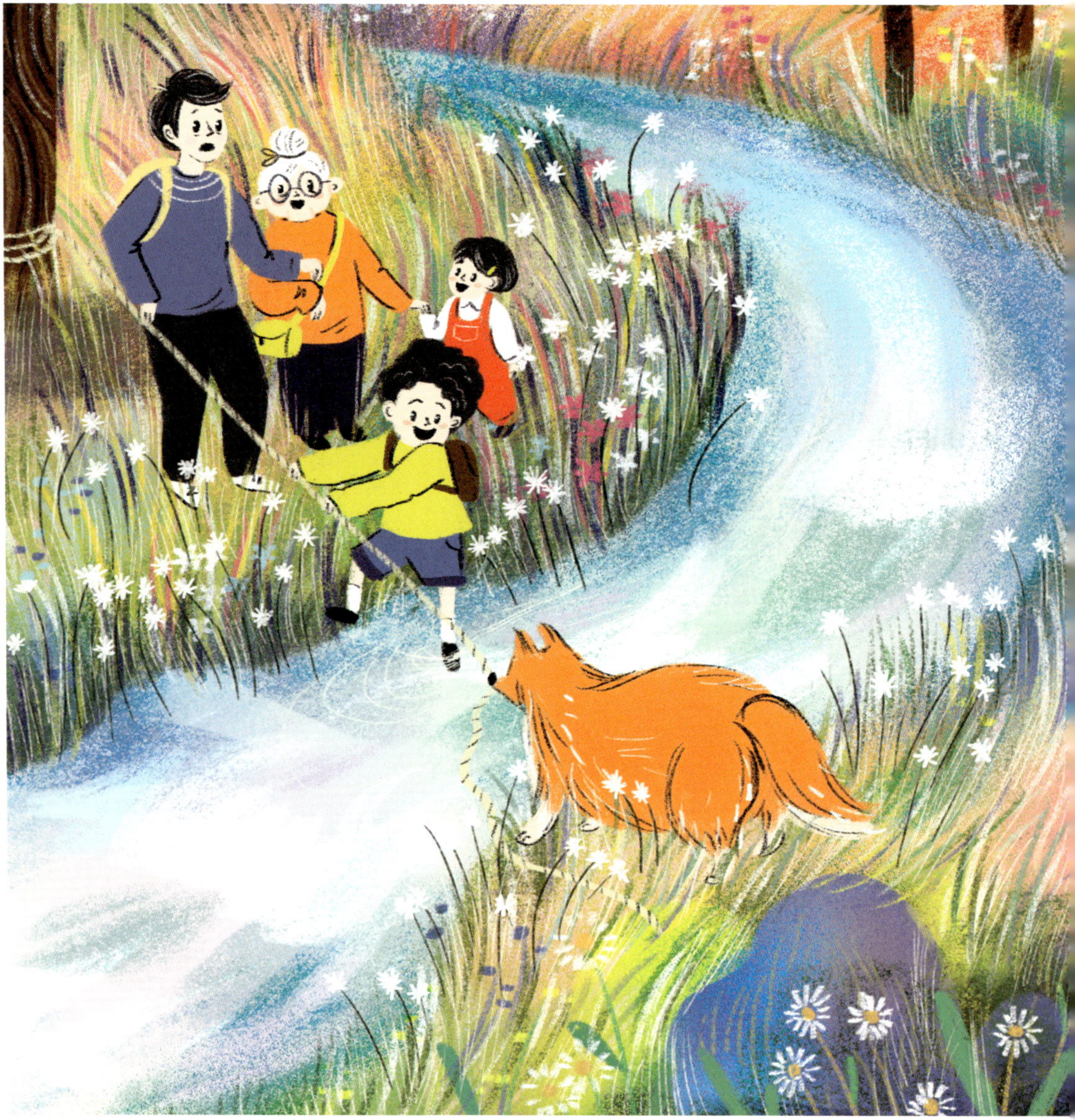

Tim did it.

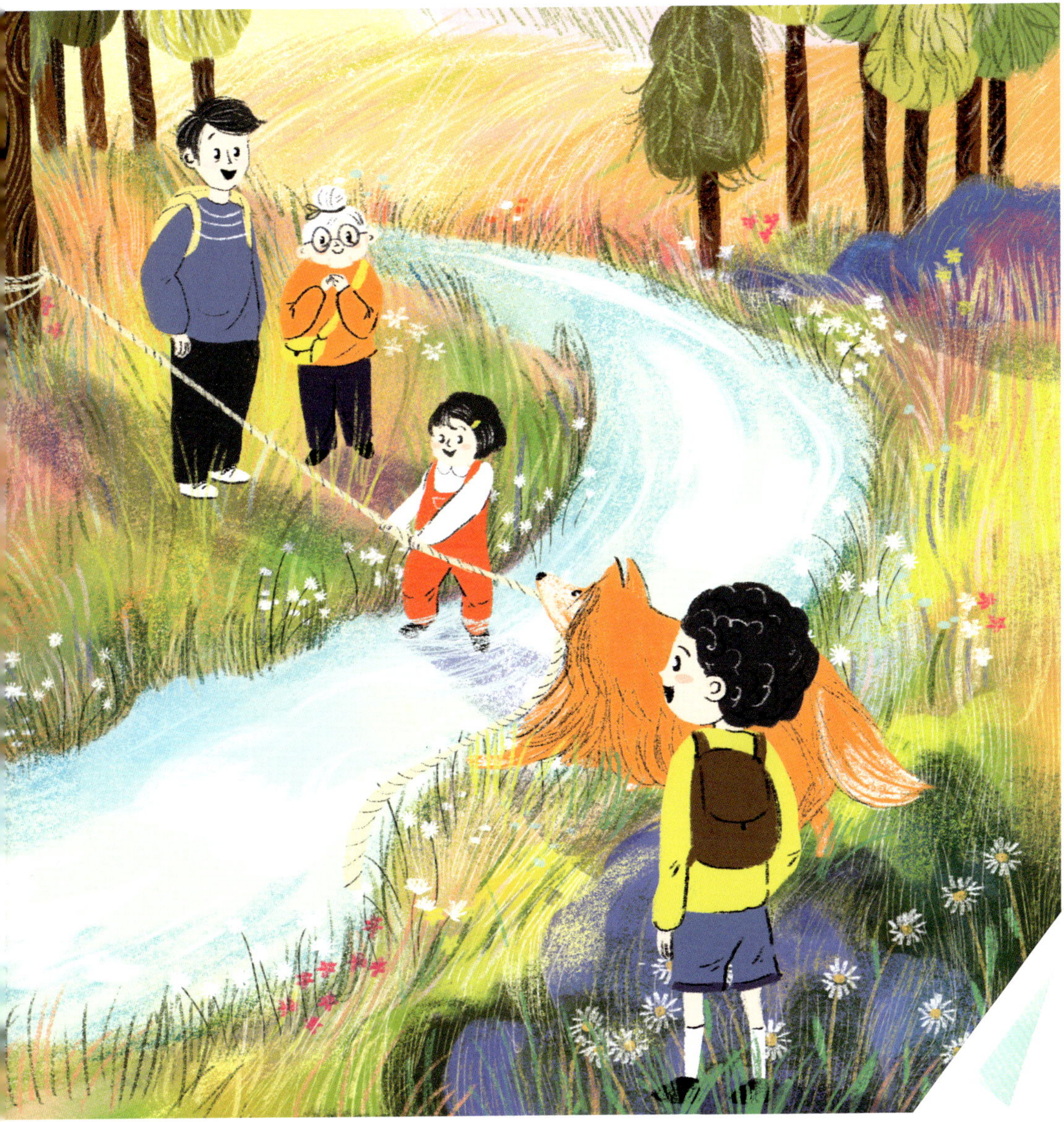

Pam did it.

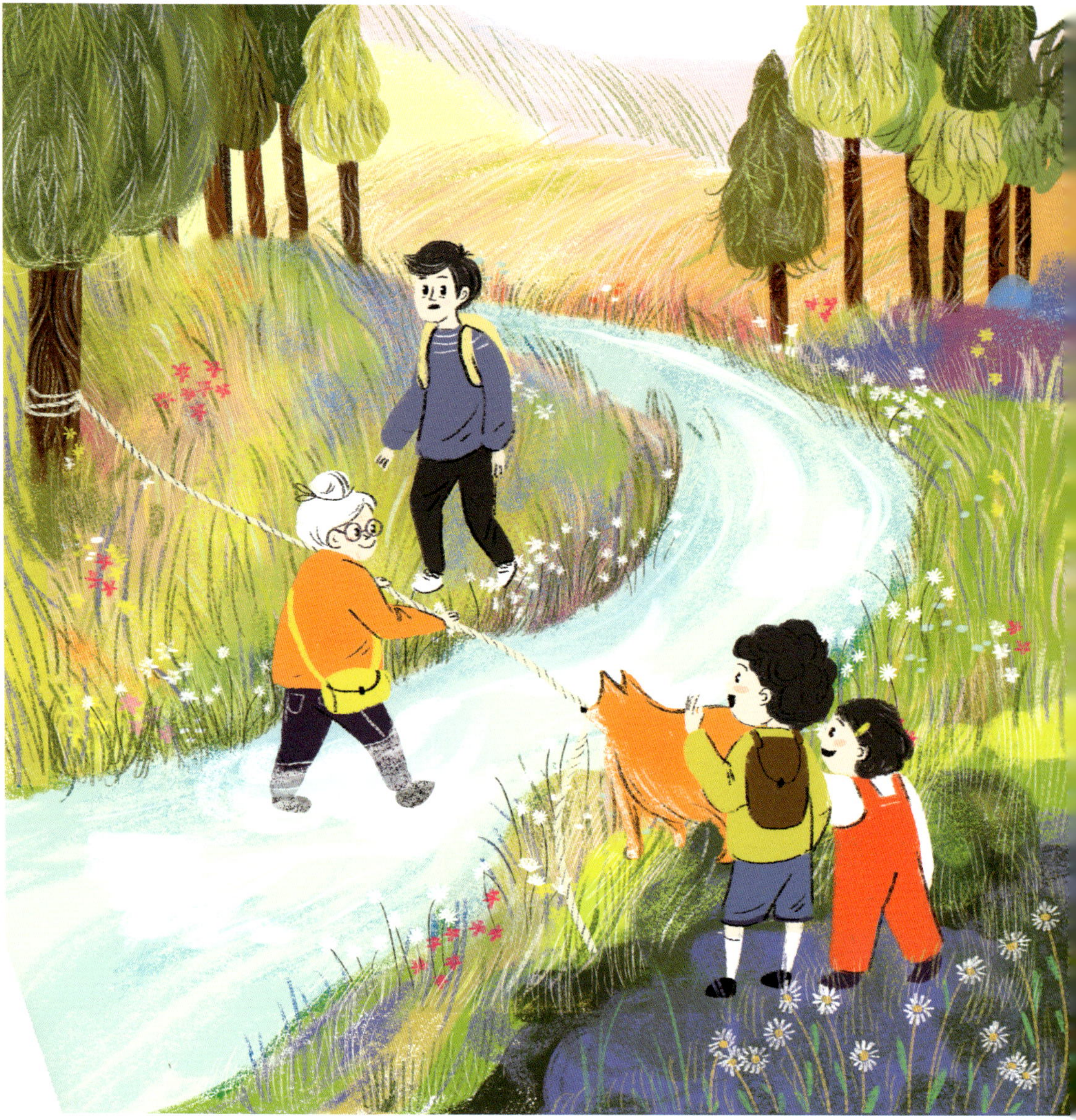

Nan did it.

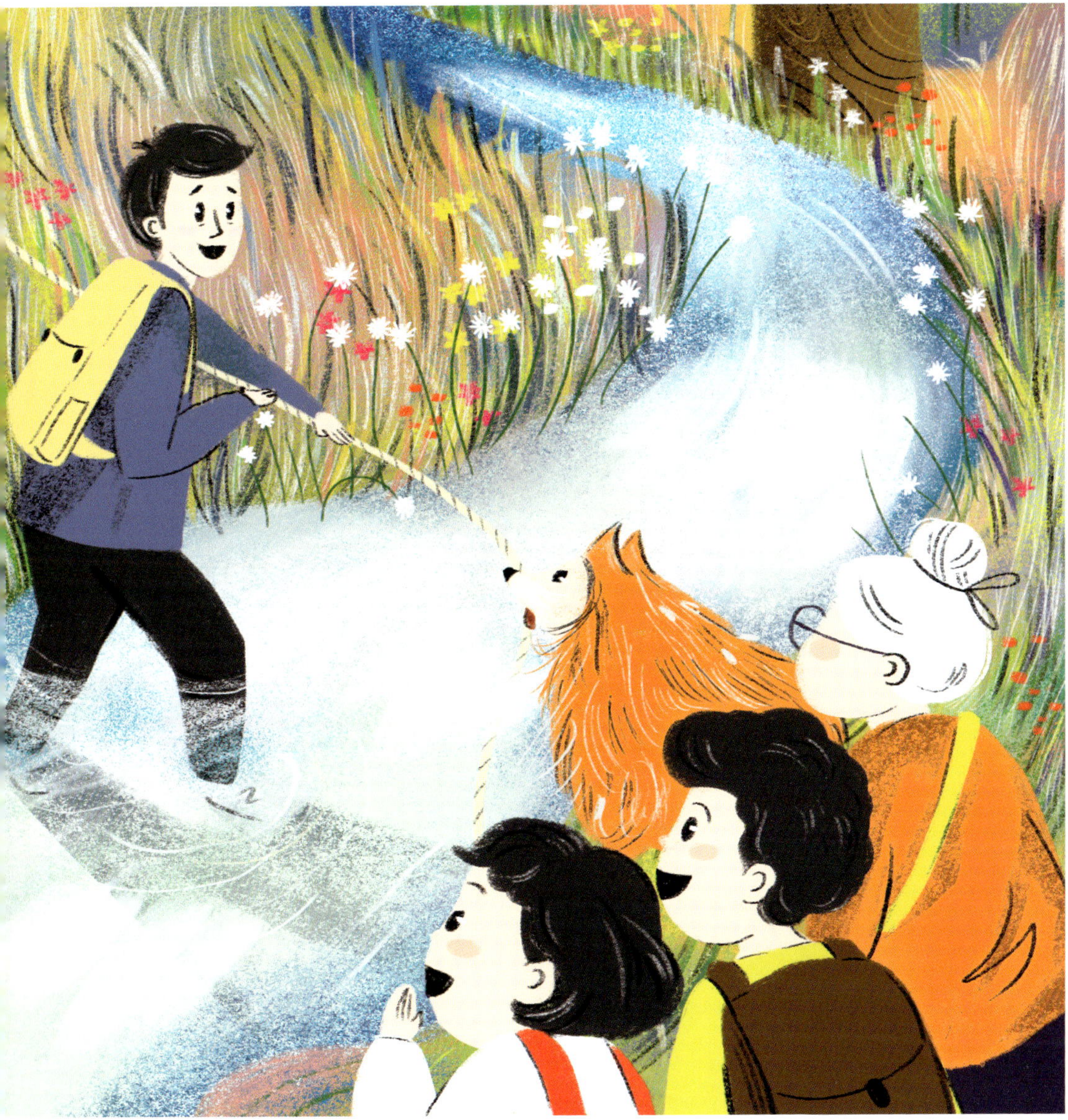

Dad did it.

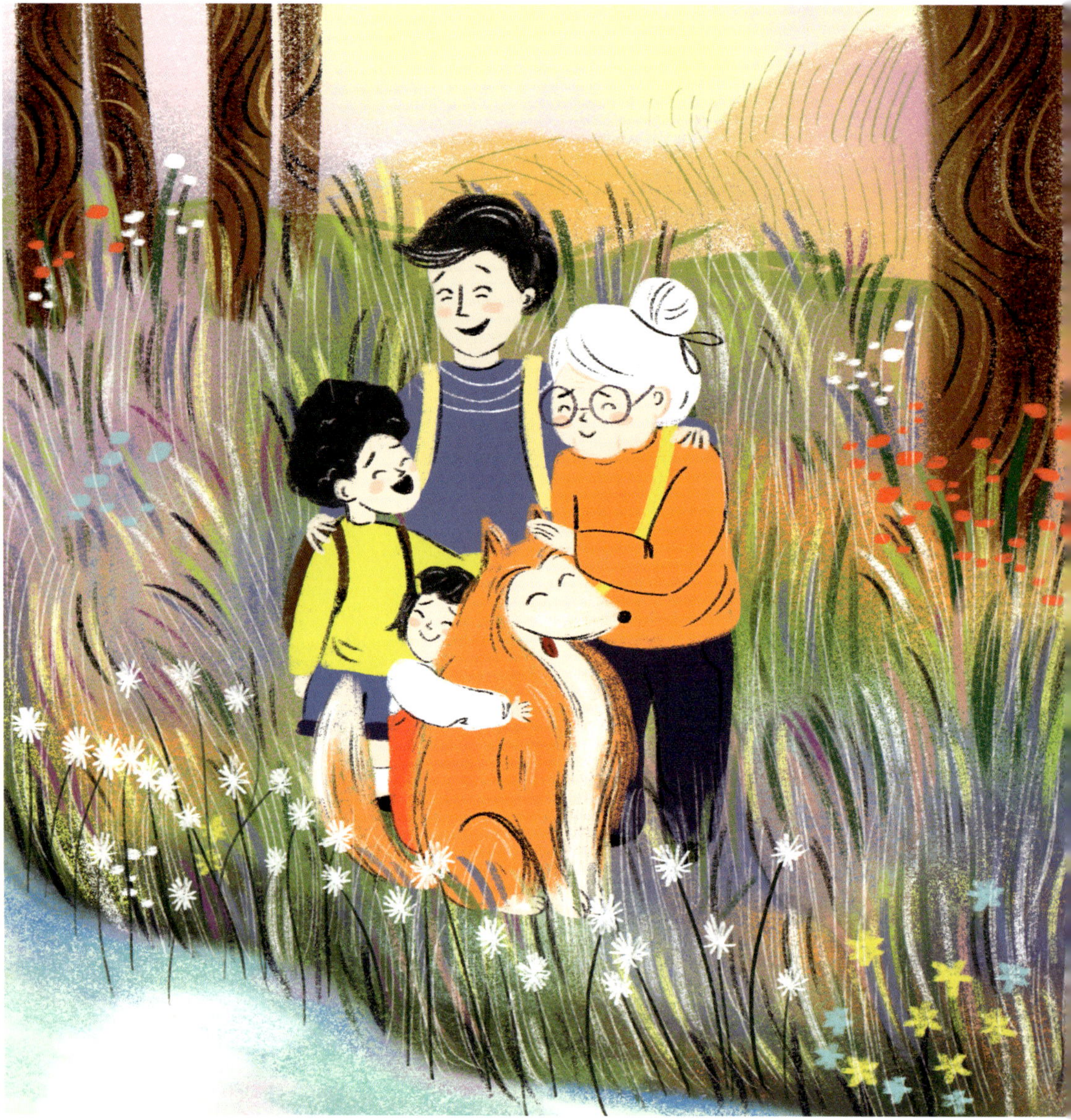

Sid did it!